FOREWORD

Take a journey through time in "Century Island", the latest in a series of locally based children's stories by the Chesapeake Mermaid. A once-vibrant bay community, teeming with oysters and healthy shorelines, was shaken by greedy pirates in search of natural resources and treasure. Realizing the damage they had done, the pirates learn from their mistakes, and work together to help restore the lands they once plundered.

As an environmental educator, it can sometimes be difficult to explain how the natural world is in trouble (and how that, in turn, affects us). "Century Island" explores complex ecological processes and timeless issues with magic and flair in a way children of all ages can understand. It touches on several valuable lessons, including owning up to your mistakes and trying to fix them. We are only one of an estimated 8.7 million species on this planet. When times are tough, the value of people of all backgrounds coming together to work towards our planet's future is an incredibly powerful image.

— *Matthew Felperin, Roving Naturalist, NOVA Parks*

1

Magical Map of the Past

Spry's Is.

Little Neck Is.

Long Marsh Is.

Three Sisters Is.

Nelson Is.

Sharps Is.

Royston's Is.

Holland Is.

Great Cove Is.

Piney Is.

Fish Is.

Century Is.

X
These are islands which have been lost. Experts estimate hundreds of islands have disappeared since the 1600s.

Map drawn with the help of John Smith, 1612.

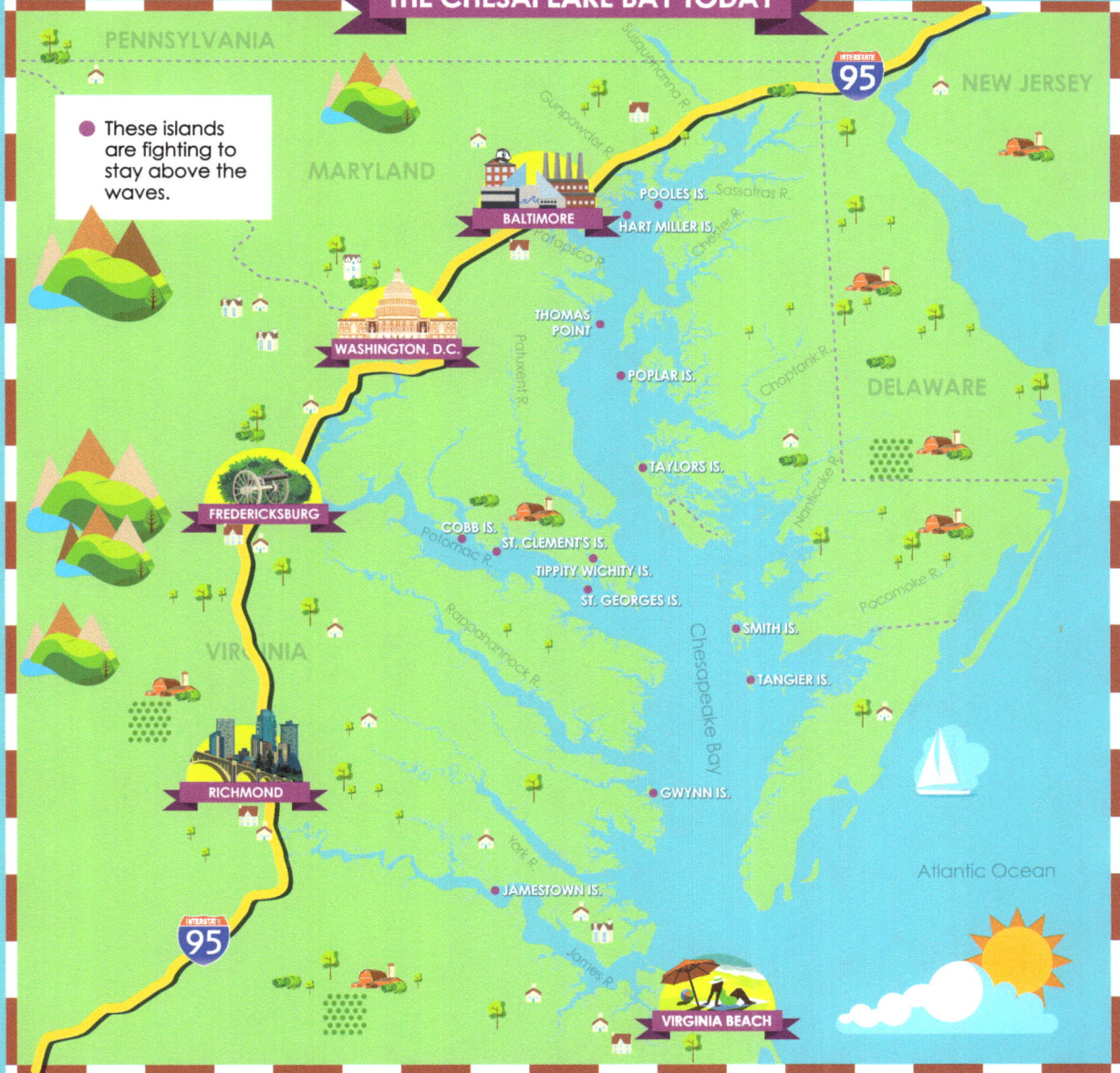

THE CHESAPEAKE BAY TODAY

These islands are fighting to stay above the waves.

PENNSYLVANIA

MARYLAND

NEW JERSEY

INTERSTATE 95

BALTIMORE

POOLES IS.

HART MILLER IS.

Sassafras R.

Susquehanna R.

Gunpowder R.

Patapsco R.

THOMAS POINT

WASHINGTON, D.C.

Patuxent R.

POPLAR IS.

DELAWARE

Choptank R.

TAYLORS IS.

Nanticoke R.

FREDERICKSBURG

COBB IS.

ST. CLEMENT'S IS.

TIPPITY WICHITY IS.

ST. GEORGES IS.

Potomac R.

Rappahannock R.

Pocomoke R.

SMITH IS.

TANGIER IS.

VIRGINIA

Chesapeake Bay

RICHMOND

GWYNN IS.

Atlantic Ocean

York R.

JAMESTOWN IS.

James R.

INTERSTATE 95

VIRGINIA BEACH

Data for vanishing islands from Cronin, W. B. (2005). *The Disappearing Islands of the Chesapeake*. Baltimore: The Johns Hopkins University Press.

3

Special thanks to my friends for their support and volunteer contributions,
my family for their endless love and encouragement,
and my sweetheart for being the best companion a mermaid could wish for.

ISBN-10: 0-9990602-5-2
ISBN-13: 978-0-9990602-5-4

4

The Chesapeake Mermaid &
Century Island

Story by The Chesapeake Mermaid

Illustrated by Angela Rose Mitchell

A long time ago, the Chesapeake Merfolk had an enchanted Marsh Organ. When played correctly, it controlled the sea level through melody by trapping the water in ice.

While the Merfolk were distracted protecting wildlife from the Storm Waters, a band of pirates took the powerful instrument to use for themselves.

The pirates moved the enchanted organ to an isolated island in the Chesapeake Bay. There, its song lowered the sea level long enough for the pirate mob to invade the bayside towns. The pirates scared the townspeople into giving them more than they needed. When there was nothing left in town to take, the pirates took from nature as well - cutting down trees, digging for gold, and feasting on oysters. They used up the natural world and left nothing behind.

Gone were the homes for people and animals. There was no longer clean water for plants to grow. There was no protection from storms. There were no longer barriers to keep the sand and soil from washing away.

The locals began to call this place the Dead Zone.

Limited to their view of the world, the pirates were blind to what was happening around them. Bay water bubbled up from within the island and the Marsh Organ fell into disrepair. The next broken tune from the organ placed a powerful curse on the island and all who lived there. The island vanished and the pirates were left to exist eternally in the Dead Zone they created.

One chance remained for these tragic buccaneers.

The island would appear from sun up to sun down once every one hundred years. During that time, the pirates would have a chance to be redeemed.

300 years passed and the Chesapeake Mermaid was swimming through the bay looking for her next adventure. She had been in the bay for 400 years helping animals in need of rescue or people who could use a friend.

In one particularly empty part of the bay, wildlife spirits called out to warn her.

"It's not safe here!"

"Turn back while you can!"

"There are dangers in the water!"

She felt an echo in the waves - a familiar song from a long, long time ago. Realizing the forlorn wildlife had been cursed by the same Marsh Organ once owned by her ancestors, she ventured onward hoping somehow she could help.

Far beneath the surface, she discovered a magical island. It was like nothing she had seen before! Over the centuries, the waves had dissolved the shoreline, the ground had sunk, and the sea level had risen. What was left of the island was now completely under water.

There, she found the cursed pirates from so many years ago.

"We have been here a long time," they shared with her, "Back then, life was very hard and we were trying to survive. We didn't need to take so much. We did it because we could. We didn't realize the damage we did would last for so long. We have seen the results of our actions, but to have the curse lifted is hopeless."

The pirates had done all they could to play the organ again or keep their island from disappearing but nothing worked. Without the balance of trees, plants, oyster reefs, and wildlife, the island could not stay above the eroding power of the waves.

The enchanted Marsh Organ could not be played under water. The pirates believed the Chesapeake Merfolk were the only ones who knew how to lift the curse. Unfortunately, all the Merfolk had left a long, long time ago...

Except for one.

"I know how to play it!" the Chesapeake Mermaid shouted excitedly.

"What if…" the mermaid thought out loud, "What if we picked up the garbage around here and reused it? We could extend the pipes above the water line. With air in the pipes again, we can play the song."

The pirates were inspired by her energy but overwhelmed by the task. "We only have ONE day…" one pirate said sadly.

"It only takes one day to make a change!" she said as she expressed with her hands. "There is a lot to be done, but it isn't hopeless. It won't be the same as it once was, but it can still be wonderful."

The pirates nodded, shook hands, and patted one another on the back. That day, the pirates learned to work together to meet their needs, each bringing their strengths to the task. They did things for one another and it felt even better than doing things for themselves.

The Chesapeake Mermaid wasn't looking well. She made more and more trips to the surface gasping for fresh air. Life was hard in the Dead Zone. Red waves of algae had stolen the oxygen from the water, making it impossible for anything to stay there for long.

With the organ pipes complete and the day growing long, she sat down to play the song. With a rumble, the fragile pipes blew a burst of bubbles into the air above the waves. The song carried through the air in swirls of magic.

But out of sight, the base of the organ began to crumble away from time and tide. The mermaid struggled to play one last song, determined to lift the pirate's curse.

One heavy piece fell onto the Chesapeake Mermaid and she was pulled deep into a cloud of debris. "Help!" she cried, expelling her last bit of fresh air. The pirates had a chance to save the organ, but instead, rushed into the chaos to help their new friend.

"We're running out of time!" one pirate shouted. "The sun is setting above!"

Working together, they smashed at the organ pieces, breaking apart all that was left, and pulled her to the surface for a fresh breath. The remaining pieces of the Marsh Organ fell into deep channels on the bay floor.

As the sunlight vanished from sight, the island dissolved and disappeared forever.

The pirates were left in the Dead Zone with no island, no enchanted organ, and no hope. The world around them was still. The sun had set and they now waited to disappear themselves. Their future? Unknown.

To their surprise, the magic in the air settled all around them. For their good deed, they were redeemed! The pirates glowed with goodness and friendship after learning to look beyond themselves. They had cared for the world as much as they cared for one another. They were no longer living for today, but for eternity. No longer cursed, they were free to move into the next world.

The mermaid was prepared to say goodbye but the pirates stopped her.

"There is a lot of work to be done here," one pirate stated, "We want to help make that happen. It's important to not cause harm, but even better to undo the harm caused by others."

The mermaid clapped and cheered because that made her so happy.

"We will remain in the Dead Zone and share our story with those who travel through here," another pirate said, "There will be more like us who think it's ok to take more than they need. We will be more generous with our world and more forgiving to one another. Perhaps we can make the future a better place."

And the future will be a better place, because **you** are in it.

Science

Sea Level

- An average level of the surface of one or more of Earth's oceans
- The average global sea level has risen since the start of the 20th century
- Predicting change is challenging because nature is complex

Marsh Organ

- Instrument of science used to study sea level change
- Shows how grasses respond differently to soil, air, and water

Dead Zone

- Areas which can not provide the basic necessities of life
- Can grow or shrink over time based on weather, pollution, and more
- Eliminating pollution, managing runoff, and regular water monitoring can help

Science

Lost Islands

- Hundreds of Chesapeake islands have been lost since the 1600s
- Islands provide predator-free habitats for wildlife like terrapins, horseshoe crabs, and migrating birds
- Some lost land is being rebuilt and habitats restored

Erosion

- The natural process of wearing down rock and soil
- Can be done by water, wind, ice, plants, animals and more

Recycle

- To make garbage into a new material or object
- May seem new but has been around for thousands of years
- Reducing what you throw away can be a better solution

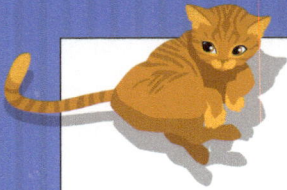

Be A Habitat Hero

- Turn off outdoor lights when you go to sleep
- Locate your nearest wildlife rescue for emergencies
- Place decals on your windows to reduce bird collisions
- Turn off the faucet when you brush your teeth
- Keep storm drains free of trash, leaves, and snow
- Respect wildlife - don't chase, shout, or get too close
- Save paper by using the back of each sheet
- Learn about endangered species in your area
- Don't let your pets live outside
- Explore rocks and sticks, but leave them where you find them
- Clean up litter (and not only your own)
- Let leaves stay where they fall
- **Follow the Chesapeake Mermaid on social media**

ABOUT THE CHESAPEAKE MERMAID

The Chesapeake Mermaid makes appearances at events throughout the region. She invites us to explore the Chesapeake watershed on a quest for innovative solutions to the natural world's toughest problems. She is a leader among volunteers and encourages the public to get involved in environmental programs. Become a part of her journey at chesapeakemermaid.com or summon her to an event by writing to info@chesapeakemermaid.com

Watch for other great adventures from The Chesapeake Mermaid

ChesapeakeMermaid.com

Forget me not is all I ask
Together we'll care for
All the animals and people
In a world that we'll restore

You and I will stay on task
A goal in life we swore
Learning is our journey now
Let's discover and explore

Forget me not is all I ask
I could not ask for more
whether standing on the west coast
Or along the eastern shore

Don't be sad about the past
what we knew is now no more
We can make the future bright
Be glad for what's in store

We can make the future bright
Be glad for what's in store